Rookie Biographies®

Sacagawea
Brave Explorer

by Jodie Shepherd

Content Consultant
Nanci R. Vargus, Ed.D.
Professor Emeritus, University of Indianapolis

Reading Consultant
Jeanne M. Clidas, Ph.D.
Reading Specialist

Children's Press®
An Imprint of Scholastic Inc.

Library of Congress Cataloging-in-Publication Data
Shepherd, Jodie.
  Sacagawea / by Jodie Shepherd.
    pages cm. -- (Rookie biographies)
  Includes index.
  ISBN 978-0-531-21414-5 (library binding) -- ISBN 978-0-531-21427-5 (pbk.)
  1. Sacagawea--Juvenile literature. 2. Shoshoni women--Biography--Juvenile
literature. 3. Shoshoni Indians--Biography--Juvenile literature. 4. Lewis and Clark
Expedition (1804-1806)--Juvenile literature. I. Title.

  F592.7.S123S54 2015
  978.0049745740092--dc23
  [B]   2015017321

Produced by Spooky Cheetah Press
Design by Keith Plechaty

© 2016 by Scholastic Inc.

Printed in China 62

SCHOLASTIC, CHILDREN'S PRESS, ROOKIE BIOGRAPHIES®, and associated logos
are trademarks and/or registered trademarks of Scholastic Inc.

1 2 3 4 5 6 7 8 9 10 R 25 24 23 22 21 20 19 18 17 16

Photographs ©: cover: Robert Schoeller; 3 top left: Vladimir Wrangel/Shutterstock,
Inc.; 3 top right: Mike Theiler/Getty Images; 3 bottom: North Wind Picture Archives;
4: Michael Haynes, www.mhaynesart.com; 7: W.H. Jackson/The New York Historical
Society/Getty Images; 11: Washington State Historical Society/Art Resource, NY; 12:
MPI/Getty Images; 15 top: Fotosearch/Getty Images; 15 bottom: National Historical
Park, Independence, Missouri, MO, USA/Bridgeman Images; 16: Ed Vebell/Getty
Images; 19: Washington State Historical Society/Art Resource, NY; 20: Washington
State Historical Society/Art Resource, NY; 23: North Wind Picture Archives; 24: Wood
Ronsaville Harlin, Inc. USA/Bridgeman Images; 28: Franz-Marc Frei/Corbis Images;
30 top left: Michael Haynes, www.mhaynesart.com; 30 top right: Mike Theiler/Getty
Images; 31 top: Washington State Historical Society/Art Resource, NY; 31 center: Ed
Vebell/Getty Images; 31 bottom: Washington State Historical Society/Art Resource, NY.

Maps by XNR Productions, Inc.

Table of Contents

Meet Sacagawea

In 1805, a young American Indian woman led a team of **explorers**. They went across thousands of miles of wilderness. Sacagawea (Sa-cah-GUH-we-ah) guided them along mountains and rivers. She helped them deal peacefully with the different people they met. And she did it all while carrying her baby on her back!

No one knows Sacagawea's exact birth date. She was born sometime between 1788 and 1790. She lived in an area that is now part of the state of Idaho. Sacagawea was a member of the Shoshone (shuh-SHOW-nee) tribe. She lived with her parents, two brothers, and a sister.

The Shoshones were wanderers. They moved from place to place, carrying their teepees with them. They hunted, fished, and gathered berries and roots.

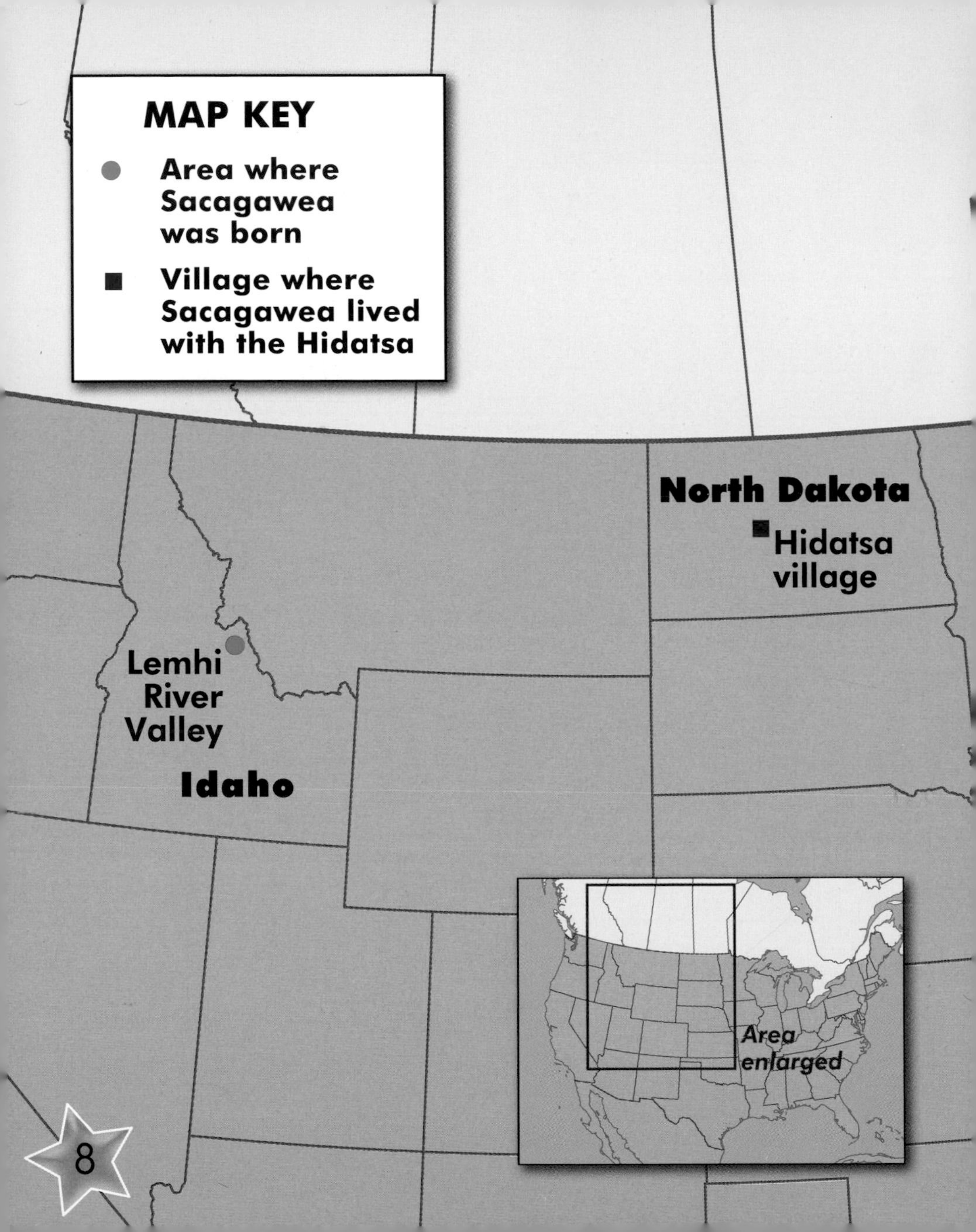

MAP KEY

● Area where Sacagawea was born

■ Village where Sacagawea lived with the Hidatsa

North Dakota

■ Hidatsa village

Lemhi River Valley

Idaho

Area enlarged

When Sacagawea was 10 or 11 years old, she was captured by Hidatsa (hee-DAHT-suh) Indians. They took her back to their own village. Her life changed completely. She began to speak Hidatsa. She learned to grow crops.

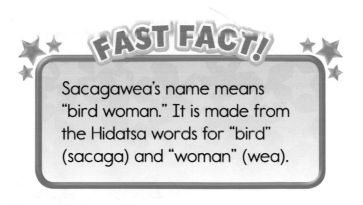

FAST FACT!

Sacagawea's name means "bird woman." It is made from the Hidatsa words for "bird" (sacaga) and "woman" (wea).

When she was 15 years old, Sacagawea married a fur trapper named Toussaint (TOO-sahn) Charbonneau (SHAR-buh-noh). Later, they had a baby boy together. Before long, this little family would start on a big adventure.

Charbonneau

The Louisiana Purchase

OREGON COUNTRY

LOUISIANA

PURCHASE

LOUISIANA TERRITORY
1805

1803

(Spain)

ILLINOIS TERR
1809

MICH TERR
1805

IND TERR
(1809)

OHIO 1803

MISSISSIPPI TERR
(1804)

ORLEANS TERR
1804

(Spain)

This map shows the land gained through the Louisiana Purchase. Most of the land to the right of that area (dark orange and light blue) already belonged to the United States. The land to the left belonged to other countries.

The Louisiana Purchase

The United States was still a new country in 1803. It was much smaller than it is today. President Thomas Jefferson believed the country should grow. So he bought a big piece of land from France. That sale was called the Louisiana Purchase. It doubled the size of the United States.

President Jefferson wanted to learn more about this new land. He chose his secretary Meriwether Lewis to head an **expedition**. Lewis asked his friend William Clark to help him lead the group of explorers.

FAST FACT!

Lewis and Clark led a group of more than 30 explorers. They called themselves the Corps (KOR) of Discovery.

Captain Meriwether Lewis

Captain William Clark

Lewis and Clark had a big job to do. They would try to find a river **route** that led to the Pacific Ocean. They would also study the people, plants, and animals they saw along the way. Finally, they would draw maps of the land as they passed through. But who could guide them through the wild country?

This painting shows the Corps of Discovery sailing on the Missouri River.

Sacagawea Sets Out

Lewis and Clark met Sacagawea when they reached North Dakota in 1804. She spoke two American Indian languages. She had lived out west and knew the land. Sacagawea was just the person to guide the expedition.

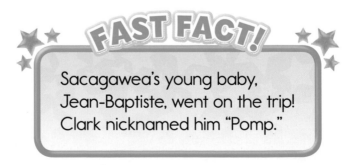

FAST FACT!

Sacagawea's young baby, Jean-Baptiste, went on the trip! Clark nicknamed him "Pomp."

The explorers headed west on April 7, 1805. Sacagawea helped guide the group. She **interpreted** American Indian languages. She helped set up camp and found roots and plants to eat. She also sewed and repaired clothing. Baby Pomp rode in a cradleboard strapped to his mother's back.

Sacagawea helped the explorers talk to people they met.

Sacagawea could be counted on in an emergency, too. One day, as the group sailed along the Missouri River, one of the boats began to fill with water. Some supplies and papers began to float away. Charbonneau froze in fear. But Sacagawea stayed calm. She rescued almost everything.

FAST FACT!

Lewis and Clark were grateful to Sacagawea. They named a river in Montana after her.

This is one of the journals from the expedition.

The group finally arrived at a place Sacagawea knew well. It was her childhood home. She was excited to see her old Shoshone friends. Even more exciting: Sacagawea's brother was now the chief of the tribe!

Sacagawea convinced her brother to help the explorers. He gave them horses to carry them through the Rocky Mountains. He sent Shoshone guides to help show them the way.

End of the Adventure

In November 1805, Sacagawea and the explorers finally reached the Pacific Ocean. They had traveled more than 4,000 miles (6,437 kilometers). And they were only half finished! They still had to make the long trip home.

FAST FACT!

In 2000, the U.S. government honored Sacagawea. They made a one-dollar coin that shows her with baby Pomp strapped to her back.

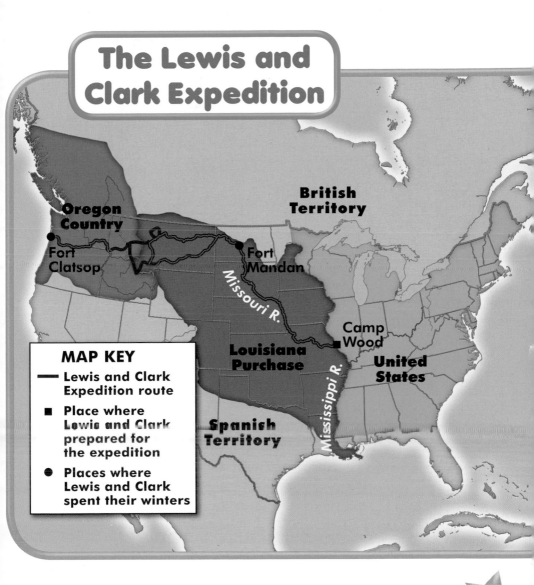

The Lewis and Clark Expedition

British Territory

Oregon Country

Fort Clatsop

Fort Mandan

Missouri R.

Camp Wood

Louisiana Purchase

United States

Mississippi R.

Spanish Territory

MAP KEY
— Lewis and Clark Expedition route

■ Place where Lewis and Clark prepared for the expedition

● Places where Lewis and Clark spent their winters

Timeline of Sacagawea's Life

sometime between 1798 and 1801
goes to live with the Hidatsa tribe

1788, 1789, or 1790
born (exact date unknown)

No one is sure how long Sacagawea lived after the trip. One thing is certain, though. It is hard to imagine the expedition without her. She was an interpreter, guide, cook, peacemaker, and more. She is one of America's earliest heroes.

1805
sets out with Corps of Discovery

1806
returns home
with her family

2000
the Sacagawea
dollar is introduced

A Poem About Sacagawea

Sacagawea hit the trail—

the only explorer who was not male!

Despite danger, hunger, snow, and hail,

with her as guide, the trip could not fail.

You Can Be an Explorer

- Do not be afraid of a challenge.
- Be on the lookout for new things to try.
- Be curious and open to adventure!

Glossary

expedition (ek-spuh-DI-shun): journey made for a specific reason

explorers (ek-SPLOR-uhrs): people who travel to discover what a place is like

interpreted (in-TUR-prit-ed): translated words from one language to another

route (ROOT): a way to travel from one place to another

Index

Facts for Now

Visit this Scholastic Web site for more information on Sacagawea:
www.factsfornow.scholastic.com
Enter the keyword **Sacagawea**

About the Author

Jodie Shepherd, who also writes under the name Leslie Kimmelman, is an award-winning author of dozens of books for children, both fiction and nonfiction. She is a children's book editor, too.

Above: Symbols. A sign of the times; Penelope and Donald choose the "Smiley" for today's group meditation. They first research the earliest meanings and interpretations of the symbol. Next they pause, slow down, and stop thinking, using the pause between their breaths to find their inner stillness. They then bring the symbol in to mind.

Above: Picking a Tarot card, like throwing runes, using the I-Ching, or scrying tea leaves, uses the fact that the inner world is reflected in the outer world to present consciousness with messages that may be acceptable. The spread above might indicate a destruction of the egoic mind by a self-revelation (The Tower), followed by a phase of innocent bliss (The Fool), leading to the development of intuitive powers (The High Priestess), and alignment to destiny (The Lovers).

THE STORY OF A LIFE
metaphor tricks and drive-thru symbols

Metaphors (from Greek *metaphora*) are close relatives of symbols that use analogies to efficiently enrich meaning. We use them all the time ("mortgage meltdown," "hit a snag," etc) without realizing just what clever tricks they can be.

For example, if "life is a journey" (a very common metaphor) then why not dream up a truly epic voyage for yourself, or at least explore what might be around the corner? In ancient shamanic traditions people often visualized, or recited, epics of travels through woods, wildernesses and caves to experience a meaningful journey and return with the resources and materials needed for a rich and successful life. The same trick still works today. Close your eyes and imagine yourself having an adventure, or guide a friend through one (try not to impose on them any of your own words or ideas—use their own words back to them). Break through walls that have barred your way, learn to *plot a course* through life.

In the ancient Chinese science of Feng-Shui the metaphor is externalized and the internal arrangement of the home and even the landscape itself are all studied as symbolic metaphors, affecting the relative probabilities of certain outcomes for the person living in that arrangement. The *perfect spot* invokes perfect dreams and a perfect life, its journey guided by a natural balance of opposites.

Metaphors are also used in high-level mind trick manipulations of mathematical and physical equations by scientists (*see below*).

*Above: A world of metaphor. Quan relaxes surrounded by a balanced
landscape, inner and outer, dreaming a happy life into being.*

SPEAK FRIEND AND ENTER
language spells and the doors they open

Doors open to friendly faces and words, so it pays to speak the language of the gatekeeper. As there are visual thinkers ("I see what you mean"), auditory communicators ("sounds right") and people who are more feelings-based ("in touch"), good speech-writers will use all the senses to connect with the most people they can.

Matching an audience's metaphors is a trick so powerful that it can unwittingly have its downside: "Don't look back!," for instance, contains the hidden command that eventually causes poor Orpheus to lose Eurydice. "Look straight ahead!" works better.

To maximize the power of language trickery use extra clean questions (*see opposite*), that minimally intrude your own words on the reality of the other person. As in hypnosis, this enables them to give full expression to their own thoughts in their own terms, solving things for themselves. Try and keep a silent mind and emotional stillness, remaining unattached to the answers.

If someone is not feeling heard, then give them their words back, perfectly repeated, or give lots of affirming "um-hums," "yeps" and "oks" as they talk. If you want to interrupt, take a deep breath and count to ten—this works anytime something rash might otherwise emerge! Another trick to get great results with your speech is to use your whole body to send your message, from stomach to nose. Good orators separate their words, round off their edges (*see below*) and time the interval between key points to fit the thinking cycle of their audience (*lower opposite*).

Above: Rich Mr. Thin shows aloof disdain for the poor
Scruffy family. They think he's an arrogant prig.

Above: Angry Mr. Fussy shows his deep sense of gratitude
for yet another beautifully served dinner.

Above: Idle Mr. Serfcrusher projects his own laziness on to
honest Bob, who had just finished a hard day's labor.

Above: Crass Mr. Deville shows his unusual sensitivity to
animal welfare on his way back from the park.

QUICK-FIX TRICKS
a useful toolkit

A stitch in time saves nine, and quick fixes have been used for thousands of years, whether mending the grass roof, or, like Caesar, rapidly adapting a battle plan to fit changing circumstances.

Complaints can be annoying. Tradesmen for centuries have dealt with them by simply staying calm, quiet, with an open body stance, good eye contact, and making notes while smiling. Medieval donkey traders probably imagined complaints splatting on the barn wall behind them. Ancient Greeks offered gifts to the Gods, to placate the difficult spirit assumed to have taken over the person, enabling both parties to blame something else for the incident, a great trick for recovering a strained relationship.

Quick fixes, while not addressing the deeper issues, nevertheless resolve many of life's problems and keep things moving. Changing clothes, *reorganizing* the layout or furnishing of a room, working in unusual places or taking some exercise all provide the context for innovative thinking and behavior. Moving to some different spaces can create fresh perspectives, allowing new insights to emerge.

If you experience an unpleasant emotion, notice where you feel it in your body. Ask yourself what might be inside the emotion. And what might be inside that? After several layers most people will arrive at a sense of inner peace or love. This is the default human condition, into which quick fixes can offer brief glimpses.

Above: Think of a problem. Notice where your eyes focus and what you imagine at that location. Turn around full circle and notice any difference. Repeat six times.

Above: Vectors. Strange though it may seem, memories are related to precise directions and distances in eye focus. A sphere of precise memories surrounds every one of us. For example, if a large spider scared you as a baby and it was up and to the left of you, then it will still be there. If today you imagine a scary spider, your eyes will again flick up and to the left. So, using this, think of a problem. Notice where your eyes go, and what might be there. You can now replace it with something pleasureable (a swish), use the spin (left), or any number of other quick fixes.

Above: A squash. Two conflicting or opposing beliefs, behaviors, or desires? Try this trick. Place one in each hand. In turn visualize and feel them until solid. Find their common higher purpose. Let them merge and bring your hands to your chest.

Left: A simple timeline trick. Identify a problem from your past. Notice where your past, present and future are, as a line on the floor. Notice the context and positive intentions of those involved. What resources might you have needed then? Step on to the line at the present point (1, opposite) and follow the sequence, gifting your younger self the resources at (3).

SYSTEMS SPELLS
changing parts to change the whole

Some fixes make things worse. Hercules cut off one of the Hydra's heads only to watch two more grow in its place. Applying a systems thinking trick he burned the stumps, thus finishing the labor.

Systems are self-contained networks, living or otherwise, exisiting within a context. Systems self-organize, generating unpredictable properties. If a system starts to produce undesirable behavior, then its structure normally needs to change. To find the best place to intervene ask "why is this happening?" and list any answers in a row. Under each answer, ask "why" again, continuing the process until patterns and sources begin to emerge. Factors can be joined by arrows showing cycles or cause–effect links (*opposite top*).

Zoom in to some typical examples of systems thinking (*below*).

Today's Problems come from yesterday's solutions

Clean up crime in one district, it will increase in another. In a complex system, cause and effect are seldom close because of the many intervening parts and delays, yet people usually assume the opposite.

The Harder you Push, the harder the System pushes back

The more hours you work, the less effective you become. Attempting superfast growth, or massive short-term gain is seldom the winning move as it stresses other parts of the system

Small changes can produce Big Results

This is because the areas of highest leverage are seldom obvious. When turning an oil tanker round, moving the rudder is too hard. Instead the rudder has a tiny rudder, called a trim tab, which is used to turn the main rudder.

The Easy Way Out usually leads back in

Low leverage interventions often appear to work in the short term. Give a man a fish and he will eat, give a man a book and he will feed himself. Give a man a trawler and his grandchildren might not end up with any fish (see opposite)

The Cure can be worse than the Disease

Sometimes the easy solution is not just ineffective, it can be addictive or dangerous. Government interventions can foster dependency. Any supposed help that weakens the host system should be suspect.

Have your Cake and Eat It but not at the same time

To have higher quality and lower costs, focus on quality systems first. Dividing an elephant in half does not produce two small elephants. Think of whole systems. Beware slow changes which cook frogs gently.

Above: Many religions, traditions, and philosophies have practices that encourage control of mind, body, and emotion, whether visualizing, praying, chanting mantras, meditating or working the body.

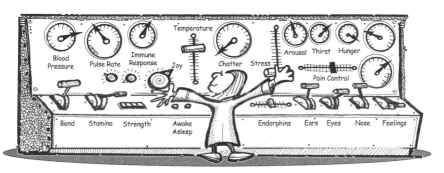

Above: Maxwell visualizes and sets the body controls for various parameters of his state, making sure he is happy and stress-free. By practicing this mind trick regularly, you can even make white skin develop melatonin.

RELEASING SPELLS
freeing the prisoners of the mind

One of the oldest tricks for many ills known worldwide is to tie a knot while thinking of a problem, and bury it. As the knot rots so the energy in the problem is released. Other ancient releasing spells involve cutting symbolic cords, purification by fire or water, and rites of passage. Laughter too, through comedy and satire, has supplied relief that has mostly kept politicians safe from the masses for eons.

Other techniques are more modern. The Fast Phobia Cure (*opposite top*) takes 10-20 minutes to scramble the access of the fear. Another trick involves grabbing the focus of attention of the person with the fear (*middle opposite*). This can resolve fears in seconds, even if more than one vectored location (*see page 25*) has to be grabbed and moved. If someone has total belief in you, just create an expectation of healing and their fear will clear instantly.

Another fast way to release stuck pains, feelings, or thoughts is to start describing them through "ings." For example "feeling paining legging footing ankling spreading shifting hurting ouching aarggh-ing phewing breathing relaxing releasing going calming fading nothing." Though it may sound strange to people around you, it works by making the experience present and ongoing so that the mind has to let go and the symptoms flow away.

Another releasing trick used for millennia is dramatic re-enactment. Examples come from grief-relieving plays in a necropolis to dream therapy, which works by reliving a dream from the point of view of each actor. Other forms have people enact the roles of significant characters, under the direction of the central character, who then experiences the drama emerging (*lower, opposite*).

Above: The Fast Phobia Cure. Antonius, terrified of snakes, watches himself nervously watching a video of his younger self being terrorized by a large serpent. Changing the color, contrast and quality of the picture transforms fear into laughter.

Above: The five-second vectored smash-and-grab phobia cure. Livia notices Caesar focusing on an imaginary scary spider, so she grabs it while he's still focused on the scary spot and removes it. Optionally she can paste something nice in its place.

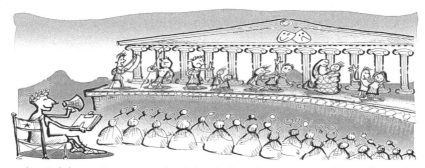

Above: Psychodramatic release. Antonius, still terrified by snakes, directs a dramatic re-enactment of the story of his terror of large serpents, no longer recoiling in horror. Members of the audience witness the events and empathize with him.

RESCALING
a trick that unravels larger knots

Long-term patterns, addictions, bad habits, and major illnesses rarely have quick fixes but require a deeper process for healing. The purpose is to attain either complete remission or acceptance.

One of the ultimate goals of Zen Buddhism [700 AD] is to be at one with the world, and the purpose of rescaling is to attain this in relation to a serious problem, moving into 1-to-1 scale with the world, seeing things as they are. It is also the condition for awakening enlightenment, or full embodiment of spirit.

This trick often works best with a friend, one of you guiding the other. The person with the problem starts scaled far out of proportion to the issue, as if seeing it through a telescope or microscope, and makes a drawing of what they see. Zooming out, they make a new drawing of the factors around the original. Progressively zooming out and making new drawings brings them to the same scale as the problem, looking out through their own eyes in a younger self that was present just before the moment that was the source of the problem. This reconnects the frozen part of the younger self back to the here and now, effecting a rapid growing up that sometimes may take a few days to integrate.

Scaling can be applied to any drawings, words, gestures, movements, nonverbal sounds, and feelings that a person might have. Ask your friend simple questions like "and does anything else go on there?", "and what could be just around that?", or "and what could be over there?" Your job is to bring their attention to spaces, actions, or words that are adjacent to, but just outside, their present focus of attention. It's easier than it sounds!

Above: Drew chooses a good place for a temple, with the right geometry of hills and water, Sun, & Moon.

Above: Drew's first successful attempt at befriending Aeolus, the ruler of the winds.

Above: Drew goes on a pilgrimage to the natural spring source of his local river.

Above: Drew studies the motions of the heavenly bodies, their influence on Earth, and how to build in tune.

Quantum Trickery
developing a new kind of mind

It is roughly one hundred years since relativity and quantum mechanics were first proposed to a skeptical scientific community, and yet very few people walking around today have any idea that the world they see is made of virtual particles, behaving in utterly strange and magical ways, or that time itself changes depending on how fast you are travelling.

These quantum laws are known to apply from the microscopic to the cosmological scale, so they apply to you and me! "In the beginning" could well be a misperception; maybe time goes backwards and forwards from now. Realizing the consciousness of every single particle and the entire cosmos, the new wizards will be those who can think equations alive, manipulating matter, space and time through pure thought.

Over 300 years ago Natural Philosophy split into science (the physically observable universe), and philosophy (the metaphysical). It is time to heal that rift, and consider consciousness, mind and matter as parts of a whole that can only be understood as one.

Whether you want to read minds, see auras or become an instant method actor, the tools are in this book—and they work. If not, ask "how come I cannot do this, yet others can?" and use some of the other tricks to address the answers! The tricks have been used for eons, they are here modernized and scientific, predictable, repeatable and observable in the mind's eye.

As the ancients knew well, "All is Mind," for the world is illusion, and seeing through the Emperor's new clothes leads to joys and worlds beyond the wildest dreams. Enjoy the now; it is all there is.